Identify a Summary

Start Here! A **summary** is a short sentence or paragraph that tells all about an object or event. A **detail** gives exact information.

👁 **Look at each picture.** 📖 **Then read the sentences.** ✏ **Write** *summary* or *detail* **to tell what each sentence is.**

1. Bob has a small blue blanket. _____

2. The puppy whined because it was cold and wet. _____

3. Bob wrapped the wet puppy in a blanket. _____

4. Bob hugged his wet puppy. _____

5. The map was torn, so Mom taped it together. _____

6. Mom has a map of the United States. _____

7. Mom found the tape in a drawer. _____

8. Mom tore the map into two pieces. _____

Go on to the next page.

Unit One: Skill Development
Summarizing 4, SV 2053-2

Identify a Summary, p. 2

📖 **Read each group of sentences below.** **Write** *summary* **or** *detail* **to tell what each sentence is.**

1. a. Abby has blue flowers in her garden. _____

   b. Abby has tall flowers in her garden. _____

   c. Abby has yellow flowers in her garden. _____

   d. Abby has many flowers of different sizes and colors in her garden.

   _____

   e. Some flowers are bigger than others. _____

2. a. Skip has red hair like his dad's. _____

   b. Skip's long, straight nose looks just like his mom's. _____

   c. Skip looks a lot like his parents. _____

   d. Skip has long fingers like his mom's. _____

   e. Skip and his dad are both of average height. _____

Unit One: Skill Development
Summarizing 4, SV 2053-2

Name _____   Date _____

Keep It Short

📖 **Read the paragraph below. Then use the words in the box to complete the summary that follows.**

Hawks, falcons, and eagles are raptors. That means they are birds that look for small animals on the ground to eat. Raptors have such keen eyesight, they can spot a small animal on the ground far below. With sharp claws called talons, they grasp the animal and carry it away as they fly high into the sky. Many raptors migrate, or move from one area to another, twice a year. These birds must move to a warmer climate when winter comes because the small animals they eat are hidden under the snow. Other animals hibernate, or go to sleep for several months. In the spring, raptors return north. There they will raise their young.

hibernate	animals	raptors	spring
talons	migrate	young	eyesight

Hawks, falcons, and eagles are **(1.)** _____. These birds

use keen **(2.)** _____ and sharp **(3.)** _____

to catch and eat small **(4.)** _____. Many raptors

(5.) _____ to warmer climates in the winter because the small

animals they eat hide under the snow or **(6.)** _____. Raptors

return in the **(7.)** _____ to raise their

(8.) _____.

Go on to the next page.

Keep It Short, p. 2

📖 Read the paragraph below. Then use the words in the box to complete the summary that follows.

Tornadoes, sometimes called twisters or cyclones, have the fastest winds on record. A tornado can whirl winds as fast as 250 miles per hour. They can tear trees up by the roots and flatten whole towns. Tornadoes most often sweep across the central plains of the United States because the land is very flat. This area is known as "tornado alley." Tornadoes almost always come in the spring. That is because during the spring, warm air from the south crashes into cooler air from the north. When that happens, thunderstorms form, and sometimes the storms cause tornadoes.

thunderstorms	towns	plains	trees
warm	tornado	cold	

The winds of a **(1.)** _____ can whirl up to 250 miles per hour. Tornadoes tear **(2.)** _____ from the ground and flatten

(3.) _____. Most tornadoes sweep across the flat land of the

central **(4.)** _____ of the United States in the spring when

(5.) _____ air from the south meets

(6.) _____ air from the

north. When that happens,

(7.) _____ form and

may cause tornadoes.

thunder storms

low air pressure
inside funnel

warm air

funnel cloud

Look for the Main Idea

A **summary** is a short statement that tells the main facts or ideas of a story.

 Circle one sentence in each story that gives the main idea.

1. Mark couldn't find his watch anywhere. He looked in the basement. He looked in the garage. Mark even looked in his brother's room. Then he finally remembered that he had left his watch at his friend's house.

2. Allan's favorite game is chess. He also likes to play checkers and backgammon. Allan likes to play card games, too. Sometimes he plays "Fish" with his friend Alex. Allan likes to play many kinds of games.

3. Mrs. Johnson was a very caring person. She always baked a cake for new people who moved into her neighborhood. She listened to the children when they asked her questions and tried to help them if they had a problem. She always offered a helping hand if she knew that someone might need it.

4. Most birds build their nests in the branches of trees. Some birds build their nests along the gutters of buildings. Birds have even been known to build nests on jungle gyms in playgrounds. You never know where you'll find a bird nest!

Go on to the next page.

Unit One: Skill Development
Summarizing 4, SV 2053-2

Look for the Main Idea, p. 2

✎ **Circle one sentence in each story that gives the main idea.**

1. There are many kinds of boats. Boats move across the water in different ways. Some people have sailboats. The wind pushes these boats to make them move. Motorboats have an engine. The engine needs gas to make a motorboat move. Other people ride in canoes. The people use paddles to move a canoe across the water.

2. One of the most common kinds of boats on a river is the barge. It is a long, low boat with a flat bottom. Barges are used to carry heavy things such as logs, sand, and cement. Most barges do not have their own engines. Instead, they are pushed by strong tugboats.

3. No harbor is complete without buoys. Buoys are floating objects that help sailors and boaters steer safely through tricky waters near shore. Some buoys show that the water is too shallow for boats. Others warn of rocks or mark the path a boat should follow. Buoys may have bells, whistles, or flashing lights.

4. A houseboat is built more for living than for sailing. Most houseboats are tied up at docks in calm waters. Although some people in North America live on houseboats, they are in much greater use in Asia. In places such as Hong Kong, where there is little land, many people live on houseboats.

Name _____   Date _____

More Main Idea

To Find the Main Idea of a Story:
1. READ the story carefully.
2. THINK about the topic of the paragraph.
3. DECIDE what all the sentences are saying about the topic.

📖 **Read each paragraph below.** ✏️ **Underline the sentence that gives the main idea. Then put a check by the sentence you would choose to be the paragraph's closing sentence. The closing sentence should repeat the main idea stated in the sentence you underlined.**

1.   The seahorse is a fish that isn't anything like a fish. It has a head like a horse and a tail that curls like a monkey's. It carries its young in a pouch like a kangaroo. It has bumps on its skin and can change color to hide from its enemies.

_____ **a.** The seahorse is not your usual fish.

_____ **b.** The seahorse got its name because it looks like a horse.

2.   The roadrunner is a flightless bird that eats rattlesnakes for dinner. It kills the rattlesnake by kicking and pecking it. How does this bird manage to avoid the rattlesnake's deadly bite? The roadrunner moves very quickly. It can run as fast as 20 miles (32.2 km) per hour and jump as high as 10 feet (3 m). So, when the rattlesnake tries to strike back with its fangs, the roadrunner can usually get out of the way in time.

_____ **a.** The most dangerous snake in the desert is the rattlesnake.

_____ **b.** This small bird is one of the rattlesnake's worst enemies.

Go on to the next page.

More Main Idea, p. 2

📖 **Read each paragraph below.** ✏️ **Underline the sentence that gives the main idea. Then put a check by the sentence you would choose to be the paragraph's closing sentence. The closing sentence should repeat the main idea stated in the sentence you underlined.**

1.   Many accidents happen on sidewalks. People may fall over toys that have been left in the way. Muddy or icy spots may cause one to slip and fall. Holes in the cement may also cause people to fall.

_____ **a.** So, be careful when walking on sidewalks to avoid accidents.

_____ **b.** So, don't step in a hole in a sidewalk.

2.   The alligator is sly when it comes to catching food. The animal dozes on the bank of the stream, appearing to be asleep. Ducks, rabbits, and other small animals may come near it. Suddenly, the alligator lashes out with its tail to kill the creature.

_____ **a.** Don't go near a sleeping alligator.

_____ **b.** Alligators trick small animals that are not careful.

3.   A tree is a very useful plant. Paper is made from wood. Medicine is made from bark. The leaves of a tree provide shade and beauty. Its roots soak up water that might have washed away soil.

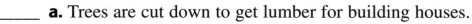

_____ **a.** Trees are cut down to get lumber for building houses.

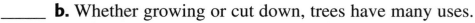

_____ **b.** Whether growing or cut down, trees have many uses.

Shorten the List

 To summarize a list of items or actions, think of one or two words that rename the list.

✎ **Fill in the blank to complete each summary.**

1.   Francine and her mother went to the mall. Francine bought two shirts. One shirt was orange, and the other shirt was blue and white striped. Francine also bought a polka dot dress. Before she left the mall, Francine bought a pair of black dress shoes. Now Francine was ready for school to start.

Before school started, Francine went to the mall and bought

_____.

2.   Lisa got out lettuce, carrots, and tomatoes. She washed and dried the lettuce. She tore the leaves and put them in a bowl. Then she cut the carrots and tomatoes. They went into the bowl, too. Then Lisa poured salad dressing in the bowl.

Lisa made a _____.

3.   Olivia went to the pet store. She saw a toucan with a long, curved bill. She also saw six blue parakeets that liked to sing. Her favorite animal was the green parrot that could say words.

Olivia saw many _____ at the pet store.

Go on to the next page.

Shorten the List, p. 2

✎ **Fill in the blank to complete each summary.**

1.   Hui signed his name at the bottom of the paper. He got an envelope and addressed the front of it. Then Hui folded the paper, put it inside the envelope, and sealed the flap. After placing a stamp on the corner of the envelope, he walked out to the mailbox to put the envelope inside. "I hope the mailman comes soon," he thought.

Hui _____ a letter.

2.   Sara went into her bedroom. It was a big mess. Clothes, books, and toys were all over the floor. First, Sara picked up her clothes. She folded them and put them in a drawer. Next, Sara put all her toys and books on the shelf. Finally, she made her bed. Sara smiled. Her room looked much better.

Sara _____ her bedroom.

3.   Jason turned off the television. He got out his math and science books. He checked his notes to see which problems the teacher assigned the class to do at home. There were many problems to work. Jason also had to write a paragraph about his favorite sport for English. Jason sighed. It would probably take all evening to get the work done.

Jason had to do his _____.

Look for Story Details

Start Here! To summarize a story, you must pay attention to the details in the story. The following questions will help you look for details:
- Who is the main character?
- Where does the story take place?
- What is the problem?

 Read the story below. Then answer the questions.

Bill was trying to save enough money to buy a football helmet. He had saved twenty dollars, but he still needed fifteen more. He walked around the neighborhood asking his relatives and neighbors if they had any jobs for him to do. Bill earned five dollars by cleaning his grandmother's garage. He earned three dollars by giving his neighbor's dog a bath. Bill weeded his mother's garden for two dollars. He cut his aunt's grass for three dollars. His father let him wash the car for two more dollars. Finally, Bill had the money! He went to the sporting goods store and bought his helmet.

1. Who is the main character?

_____

2. Where does the story take place?

_____

3. What is the problem?

_____

Go on to the next page.

Look for Story Details, p. 2

Read the stories below. Then answer the questions.

1.   Mrs. Wilson had been in the hospital for a week. Finally, she was able to come home. The neighbors planned a surprise party to welcome Mrs. Wilson back. Children blew up balloons and tied them to the mailbox. Someone put baskets of flowers by the front door. Another person had painted a huge banner that said, "Welcome home, Mrs. Wilson!" Everyone brought food, cards, and presents. Mrs. Wilson was so surprised. She thanked everyone for making her feel special.

   a. Who is the main character?

   _____

   b. Where does the story take place?

   _____

   c. What is the problem?

   _____

2.   Greg was furious. A group of boys had invited Greg to go to the movies with them, but Greg's mother had said he couldn't go. She did not like the idea of boys his age going to a movie without an adult. Greg sat in his room all night and thought about how angry he was at his mother. He also thought about how embarrassed he would feel when he saw his friends again.

   a. Who is the main character?

   _____

   b. Where does the story take place?

   _____

   c. What is the problem?

   _____

More Story Details

Start Here! To summarize a story, you must pay attention to the details in the story. The following questions will help you look for details:
- Who is the main character?
- Where does the story take place?
- What is the problem?

📖 Read the story below. Then answer the questions.

Carl had just finished putting his clothes in the closet. He liked his new room. It was big enough to hold his bed, dresser, desk, and a bookshelf. He liked the new house, too. It was much bigger than the old one. He did not have to share a room with his brother, either. Carl heard some people laughing in front of the house. He turned to look out the window. Carl saw some children about his age riding bikes. He hoped he could make friends soon. Maybe if he went outside now, he could meet some of those children. Carl raced out of his room to go find his bike.

1. Who is the main character?

_____

2. Where does the story take place?

_____

3. What is the problem?

_____

Go on to the next page.

More Story Details, p. 2

📖 Read the stories below. Then answer the questions.

1.   Maureen sat quietly on the big yellow school bus.
She could hardly believe she was going to be in fifth
grade this year. She was very excited. But she was
nervous, too. The fifth grade was in a different school. The students in her class
would be the youngest students in the school. She wondered if the older students
would make fun of the younger ones. At the same time, Maureen thought it would
be fun to be in a new school with older students. Her stomach was full of butterflies!

a. Who is the main character?

_____

b. Where does the story take place?

_____

c. What is the problem?

_____

2.   Everything had gone just as planned. As soon as the bell rang, the students sat
in their seats. Mr. Clark had no idea that something special was about to happen.
Lisa asked for permission to be excused. Mr. Clark said she could. When Lisa
came back in, she was carrying a birthday cake with candles on it. The class
started singing "Happy Birthday." Mr. Clark was very surprised. Tommy got some
plates and forks from the cafeteria. Everyone enjoyed the birthday cake.

a. Who is the main character?

_____

b. Where does the story take place?

_____

c. What is the problem?

_____

Story Outlines

 Start Here! An **outline** can be used to help summarize a story. It groups a list of items together. The heading of each part of the outline is the main idea. Main ideas have Roman numerals before them. The items underneath list the important details, or subtopics. Capital letters are used for subtopics.

✍ **Fill in the outlines below. Follow the directions given for each part.**

A. Below are four main topics. Write each main topic in a blank so that it fits the facts (subtopics) below it. The first one is done for you.

> Ways of transporting coal
> Formation of coal
> Types of mines
> Preparing coal

I. Formation of coal

   A. Plant life died and rotted

   B. Pressure was applied

II. _____

   A. Surface

   B. Underground

III. _____

   A. Remove rocks

   B. Make pieces smaller

   C. Wash

IV. _____

   A. Railroads

   B. River barges

B. Below are some facts (subtopics) about rabbits. Write the facts (subtopics) on the lines under the main heading each one fits.

> Feed at night,
> Jackrabbit, Long ears,
> Kick and bite, Sharp teeth,
> Cottontail, Strong hind legs

I. Appearance of rabbits

   A. _____

   B. _____

   C. _____

II. Habits of rabbits

   A. _____

   B. _____

III. Kinds of rabbits

   A. _____

   B. _____

Go on to the next page.

Story Outlines, p. 2

📖 **Read the story. Then follow the directions for making an outline.**

Planting a Garden

First, choose a spot of ground where plants will grow well. The ground should be fairly fertile. It should get plenty of sunshine. Pick a spot where you can bring water to the plants.

After you have chosen a garden spot, get the soil ready for planting. Scatter fertilizer over the ground. Next, dig up the ground and break up any large clumps of dirt. Then, rake the soil until it is fine and the garden plot is level.

Now you are ready to plant some seeds. Dig the holes in straight rows. Place seeds an equal distance apart as the seed package shows. Cover the seeds with soil. Water the garden if it does not rain. Soon you should have some plants.

Follow these directions for making an outline.

1. Look at the first sentence of each paragraph to find the main idea. Write a main idea after each Roman numeral.

2. Write other facts on the lines below the main idea.

3. Begin each line with a capital letter.

I. _____

   A. _____

   B. _____

   C. _____

II. _____

   A. _____

   B. _____

   C. _____

   D. _____

III. _____

   A. _____

   B. _____

   C. _____

   D. _____

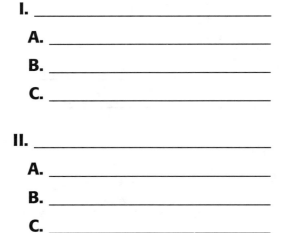

Unit One: Skill Development

Summarizing 4, SV 2053-2

Story Webs

Start Here! A **story web** can be used to help summarize a story. It is a drawing that shows the main idea written in a circle. The details are written around the main idea.

Read the story. Then complete the story web. One detail has been written in for you.

A mountain goat is especially equipped for climbing. Its two-toed hooves help it grip steep rocks. A rough pad under each toe helps the goat hang onto slippery surfaces. Each toe also has a pointed tip that is good for gripping small cracks in a mountainside. A mountain goat's short legs also help it keep its balance.

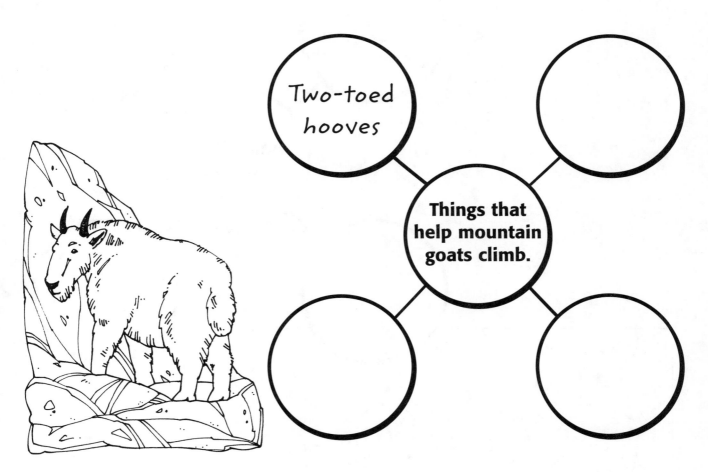

Go on to the next page.

17

Story Webs, p. 2

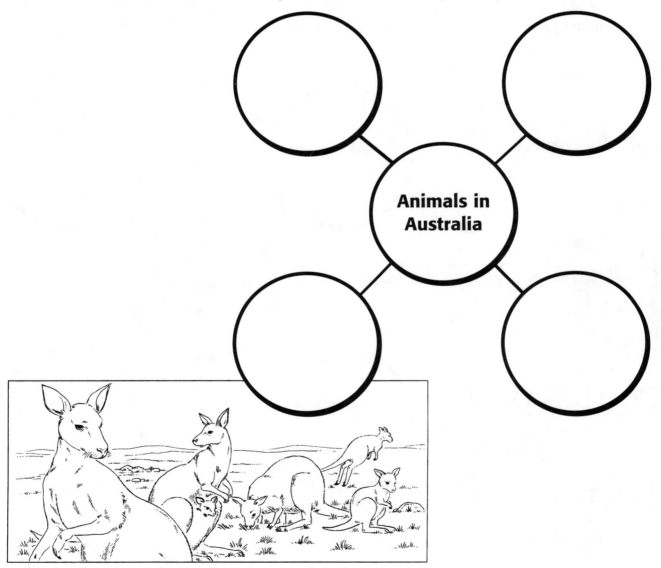

📖 **Read the story. Then complete the story web.**

There are many interesting animals that live in Australia. Kangaroos are native to Australia. They carry their baby kangaroos, called joeys, in a pouch. Australia is also the home of a huge bird, the emu. The emu is only a little smaller than an ostrich. It eats grass, flowers, insects, and almost anything else. Another strange animal from Australia is the platypus. It looks like a combination of a beaver, a duck, and an otter. Another animal there, the koala, lives mostly in trees. It looks like a stuffed teddy bear and moves very slowly.

Animals in Australia

Unit One: Skill Development
Summarizing 4, SV 2053-2

Story Maps

Start Here! A **story map** can be used to help summarize a story. It is a chart that shows the main parts of a story. A story map usually tells about the main character, the setting, and the important parts of the plot, or events in the story.

Read the story. Then complete the story map.

Georgia wanted a certain striped shirt she saw in a store window. Her birthday was in several days, so Georgia's sister said she would buy the shirt as a gift. Georgia described the shirt and told her sister where to get it. When her birthday came, Georgia eagerly opened her sister's present. Her sister watched in satisfaction. Imagine Georgia's surprise when the shirt in the box was not the one she wanted. Georgia knew her sister had gone to a lot of trouble, and she didn't want to hurt her feelings. Georgia said thank you and gave her sister a big hug.

Main Character	Setting	Plot

Go on to the next page.

Unit One: Skill Development
Summarizing 4, SV 2053-2

Story Maps, p. 2

 Read the story. Then complete the story map.

Ken was watching his neighbor's dog, Phil, the other day. Phil got away. The neighbor said Ken should always keep a leash on Phil, but Phil was being so good, Ken didn't think the dog would run away. Boy, was Ken wrong! Phil saw a cat, and he was off in a flash. Ken looked for the dog for an hour. Ken felt awful that he had let his neighbor down. Ken wished he could just snap his fingers,  and Phil would appear beside him. As it turned out, Phil came back on his own. He had rolled in something that smelled bad, but he was back! Ken was so happy to see Phil, he didn't mind getting soaked while giving the dog a bath.

Main Character	Setting	Plot

Story Frames

Start Here! A **story frame** can be used to help summarize a story. It is a brief paragraph that tells the main parts of a story. A story frame usually tells about the main character, the setting, and the important parts of the plot, or events in the story.

📖 **Read the story. Then complete the story frame.**

Fox was walking through the woods. He saw some grapes on a vine. How delicious they looked! He decided to have some grapes for his lunch. The grapes were quite high, and it was hard for Fox to reach them. He stretched and jumped, but he could not get the grapes. Fox tried again and again. The grapes always seemed just out of reach. Finally, Fox gave up. He walked away, asking himself, "Who would want those sour old grapes?"

(1.) _____ was walking through the

(2.) _____. He saw some **(3.)** _____.

Fox wanted the grapes for his **(4.)** _____. He tried to get the

grapes, but he could not reach them. Fox finally gave up and walked away,

saying the grapes were **(5.)** _____.

Go on to the next page.

Story Frames, p. 2

📖 Read the story. Then complete the story frame.

The first handkerchiefs were used in ancient Rome. Only rich people could afford these white linen cloths, and they used them mainly for wiping their brows. When it became cheaper to make these cloths, ordinary Romans used them, too. They often waved their handkerchiefs as a way of greeting important people or applauding for actors in the theater. In later centuries, handkerchiefs were very beautiful and were carried for display. Sometimes women gave a handkerchief to a man as a sign of affection.

Handkerchiefs were first used by early **(1.)** _____ of wealth

to mop their **(2.)** _____. Later, common citizens of Rome used

(3.) _____ to **(4.)** _____ at important people.

In more recent centuries, handkerchiefs were carried for **(5.)** _____

or given as signs of **(6.)** _____.

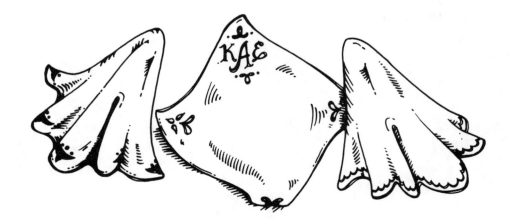

Sum It Up

Start Here! When you tell a short form of a story, you are making a **summary**. A summary is a short account of the main idea and important details. There are some things that you leave out of a summary. That is because they are less important than the main idea and important details. They may make the story more interesting, but you can tell the story without them.

📖 **Read the story and think about how you would tell the main idea and important events in a few sentences.**

Tommy couldn't find his baseball glove anywhere. He hadn't used it since last spring when his team played in the tournament. He looked in his closet. He looked under his bed. He looked in his brother's bedroom. Finally, he asked his mother if she knew where the baseball mitt was. She said it was right where he had left it. It was in the basement on the game shelf.

Before you can retell this story in a few sentences, you must decide what are the most important parts of the story. For this story, you would probably write a summary like this:

Tommy couldn't find his baseball glove, but he finally found it in the basement.

Go on to the next page.

Sum It Up, p. 2

 Start Here!

To Summarize a Story:
1. READ the story carefully.
2. THINK about its main idea and important details.
3. INCLUDE only those ideas in your summary.

 Read each story. **Then write a summary using complete sentences.**

1.　　Ron was having a good time. He liked to watch the animals eat. He was glad he had come to the zoo in time to watch the animals get fed. They were much more active during feeding time.

_____

_____

2.　　Janet decided it was time to plant her garden. She went to the garden shop and bought some seeds. She got her tools from the garage. She went to her garden spot and started breaking up the ground. She made rows and planted lettuce, onions, tomatoes, and green peppers.

_____

_____

3.　　Diane woke up early. She had several things to do today. She had to clean her room. Then she was going to a birthday party. Later she had a flute lesson. That evening she was going out to eat and to a movie with her parents.

_____

_____

Name _____ Date _____

More Summaries

 Start Here!

To Summarize a Story:
1. READ the story carefully.
2. THINK about its main idea and important details.
3. INCLUDE only those ideas in your summary.

 Read each story. **Then write a summary using complete sentences.**

1. Whenever someone needed to know how to spell a word, they always asked Juanita. Some of her friends called her a "walking dictionary." She had won the annual spelling bee at school for the past three years.

_____

_____

2. Judy likes the meadow. In the spring, it is full of new life and the smell of new grass. In the summer, it is full of life and pretty flowers. In the fall, the meadow is surrounded by trees of all colors. In the winter, the meadow is a great place for walking. Judy loves to come to the meadow in all the seasons.

_____

_____

3. Paula has a dog named Jupiter. Jupiter is really smart. He can sit up. He can also play dead. When she tells him to, Jupiter will stay where he is until Paula says that he can move. The dog also can jump through hoops and over fences.

_____

_____

Go on to the next page.

Unit Two: Practice
Summarizing 4, SV 2053-2

More Summaries, p. 2

 Read each story. **Then write a summary using complete sentences.**

1.   The meadow is full of all kinds of animal life. Insects buzz around flowers. Little rabbits hop in the tall grass. Birds sing in the trees as they build nests. Mice and moles make their homes in the meadow, too.

_____

_____

2.   Terry likes to read mysteries. She also enjoys books that make her laugh. Her favorite books are about horses. When Terry goes to the library, she has a hard time choosing which book she will read that week.

_____

_____

3.   Wesley has a sister that is one year old. Wesley likes to rock his baby sister to sleep. He enjoys feeding his sister. His mother even taught him how to change the baby's diaper. Wesley's favorite thing to do is to play with his sister while his mother is busy doing other things.

_____

_____

4.   It was Ana's birthday. William gave her a ring with a red stone. Inga gave her a game. Max gave her a book about horses. Ana's mom gave her a guitar and music lessons. Ana tried to play the guitar, but made funny noises with it. Everyone laughed. It was good that Ana got lessons to learn how to play the guitar.

_____

_____

Long Story Summary

Start Here! When writing a summary of a long story, look for the main idea and important details. Then write four or five sentences to summarize the story.

📖 Read the story. ✏️ **Then write a summary using complete sentences on the next page.**

It's How You Look at It

Betty's family moved into the house by the highway in the fall. The back of the house looked out over a little meadow. Beyond the meadow was a forest. The forest trees grew on a steep hill that ran down to a creek. On the other side of the creek was another hill.

Betty became very interested in the lights she could see glowing from a house on the far hill. At night the house had many shining windows. As the leaves fell off the trees, she could see more of it; but she could not tell much about it. "It must be very grand," she thought. "It must be a much bigger house that our new home. I wonder who lives in such a grand house."

One evening Betty and her father got in the car and found the narrow road the other house was on. They had trouble deciding which house was the one Betty had seen. "None of the houses on this road looks so special up close," she said. Then all at once she exclaimed, "This is the house. I know because I can see our house across the valley. But our house looks much bigger from here."

The Sun was setting, and it reflected off the windows of Betty's new house. "Look!" she cried. "Our house has golden windows!" On the way home, she thought about the people who lived in the house she had seen. "They must look over at us and wonder who lives in the special house with the golden windows," she thought.

Go on to the next page.

Long Story Summary, p. 2

Think about the story you read.  **Write four or five sentences that summarize the story. Remember, a summary does not tell all the details, but tells the main points of the story.**

Summary and Story Webs

Start Here! A **story web** can be used to help summarize a story. It is a drawing that shows the main idea written in a circle. The details are written around the main idea.

📖 **Read the story. Then complete the story web. One detail has been written in for you.** ✏️ **Write a summary using complete sentences.**

People who plan to camp should be prepared for some crawly company. Spiders surprise campers by appearing in unusual places. Spiders can be found on early morning canoe trips. They might jump out of boots, drop from trees, or crawl out from under rocks. Campers should expect to find spiders in tents, woodpiles, and even in backpacks.

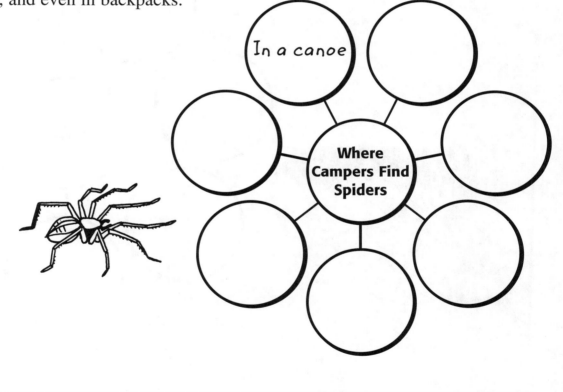

_____

_____

_____

Go on to the next page.

Summary and Story Webs, p. 2

Read the story. Then complete the story web. Write a summary using complete sentences.

What has fur and wings, flies at night, and sleeps upside down during the day? A bat, of course! Bats are the only flying mammals. They live in large groups, called colonies. During the warmer months, at dusk each day, the entire colony will take wing at once. They fly in swarms from their upside-down perches in search of insects. One bat can eat up to 1,000 insects an hour.

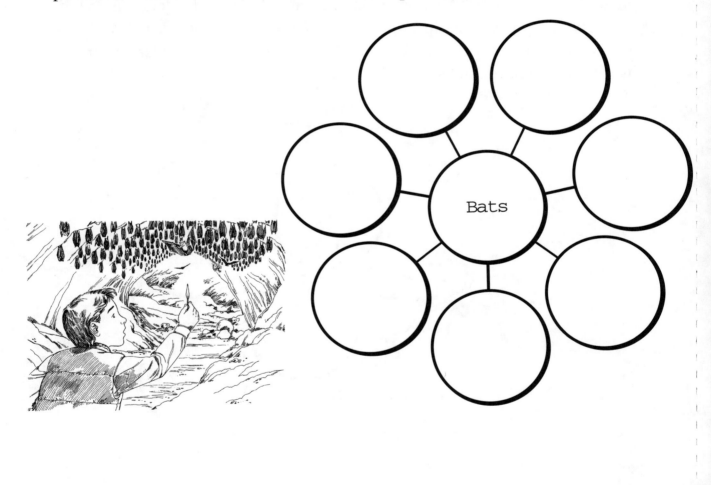

Bats

_____

_____

_____

Summary and Story Maps

Start Here! A **story map** can be used to help summarize a story. It is a chart that shows the main parts of a story. A story map usually tells about the main character, the setting, and the important parts of the plot, or events in the story.

📖 **Read the story. Then complete the story map.** ✏️ **Write a summary using complete sentences.**

Miss Trinidad had lost her glasses. She wanted to read a book and needed the glasses to be able to see it. Miss Trinidad hunted all over the house. She started in the bedrooms and ended up looking in the kitchen. She even looked in the garbage can. Finally, in exasperation, she put her hand to her head. Miss Trinidad smiled. What a silly mistake she had made! The glasses had been on her head the whole time.

Main Character	Setting	Plot

Go on to the next page.

Summary and Story Maps, p. 2

📖 **Read the story. Then complete the story map.** 🖊 **Write a summary using complete sentences.**

Marilu and her grandpa wanted to build a birdhouse for the chickadees that came calling. They knew a small house would be good for chickadees, but they wanted to build the house just right. So Marilu and her grandpa read a book on building birdhouses. They also asked the advice of Mr. Lopez, a neighbor who already had built several birdhouses. He said to be sure that the birdhouses could be opened so they could be cleaned. He also offered to let them use his hammer, saw, and some wood. Marilu and her grandpa had fun making the birdhouse in Marilu's garage. Now they enjoy watching the chickadees come and go from their new home.

Main Character	Setting	Plot

Summary and Story Frames

Start Here! A **story frame** can be used to help summarize a story. It is a brief paragraph that tells the main parts of a story. A story frame usually tells about the main character, the setting, and the important parts of the plot, or events in the story.

Read the story. Then answer the questions.

Lindsey and her friend Kate had gone to the mall. Lindsey's mom agreed to let them walk around by themselves, but they needed to meet her by the fountain at 5:00. The girls had walked all over and gone into several stores. Lindsay's favorite store was a candle shop. The candles had different smells and shapes. They were having a great day. The girls were having such a good time that they didn't realize it was time to meet Lindsay's mom. They were surprised when they saw a clock that showed 5:00, and they had to go home.

1. Who is the story about? _____

2. Where does the story take place? _____

3. What happens in the story? _____

_____

Write a summary using a story frame. Be sure to write complete sentences.

_____

_____

_____

Go on to the next page.

Summary and Story Frames, p. 2

📖 Read the story. Then answer the questions.

Megan had been saving her allowance for some time. The last time she had checked, she had $10.85. Just last week she had seen a tennis racket at Gord's Sporting Goods Store. It was on sale for $13.99. With this Saturday's allowance, she would have $12.85. She really wanted that racket. Megan was thoughtful for a moment, then she sprang into action.

Soon she was sweeping out the garage and organizing the garden tools. When she finished that job, she began to weed the garden. When Megan's parents saw what Megan had done, they each gave her a dollar for all the extra work she had done. Megan counted her money again. Then she started skipping down the street in the direction of the sporting goods store.

1. Who is the story about? _____

2. Where does the story take place? _____

3. What happens in the story? _____

_____

✏️ Write a summary using a story frame. Be sure to write complete sentences.

_____

_____

_____

Newspaper Summary

Start Here! A **story frame** is a brief paragraph that tells the main parts of a story. A story frame usually tells about the main character, the setting, and the important parts of the plot, or events in the story. The first paragraph of most newspaper stories uses a story frame.

Read the story. Then answer the questions. **On the next page, write a newspaper article that summarizes the story below.**

Three goats lived in a meadow. They looked up one day and noticed that the grass across the river was much greener. Yum! Little Billy Goat Gruff decided to cross the bridge to eat the grass. As he stepped onto the bridge, a troll growled, "I'm going to eat you!"

Little Billy Goat Gruff answered in a shaky voice, "My brother is coming, and he is much bigger than me." The troll let the little goat pass. The troll wanted a bigger goat.

Middle Billy Goat Gruff began to cross the bridge. The troll growled, "I'm going to eat you!"

Middle Billy Goat Gruff answered in a shaky voice, "My brother is coming, and he is much bigger than me." The troll let the middle goat pass. The troll wanted a bigger goat.

Big Billy Goat Gruff began to cross the bridge. The troll growled, "I'm going to eat you!"

Big Billy Goat Gruff answered in a strong voice, "I think you will go hungry today." He used his big horns to push the troll off the bridge. The goats spent a beautiful day eating green grass. The troll never bothered the goats again.

1. Who is the story about? _____

2. Where does the story take place? _____

3. What happens in the story? _____

_____

Go on to the next page.

Name ______________________ Date ______________

Newspaper Summary, p. 2

Write a newspaper article that summarizes the story on the first page. Be sure to use a story frame that tells the main characters, setting, and story events.

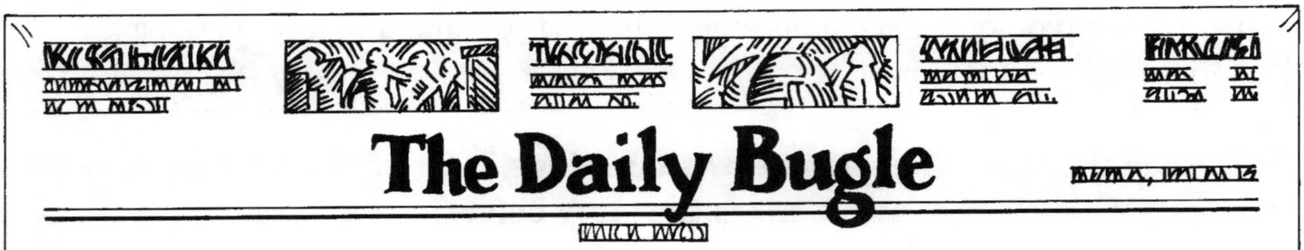
The Daily Bugle

____

____

____

____

____

____

____

____

____

____

____

Name _____   Date _____

Summarizing: Test 1

📖 **Read each story. Then read the answer choices.** ✏️ **Fill in the answer circle in front of the best summary of the story.**

As Melissa got ready for the first day of school, she thought about all that had happened that summer. She had broken her leg early in June. It had seemed as if the summer was going to be ruined because she couldn't go swimming. Then she had started going to the Youth Club, which had science and craft centers, as well as a swimming pool. She had a wonderful time and had learned about many new things.

1. Which of the following is the best *summary* of the above story?
Ⓐ Melissa had spent most of the winter at the Youth Club.
Ⓑ Even though Melissa broke her leg, she had a good summer.
Ⓒ Melissa broke her leg early in the summer.
Ⓓ Melissa got ready for the first day of school.

Steve had worked very hard on his exhibit for the fair. He was going to enter the photography contest. He had taken over a hundred pictures during the summer. It had been hard to choose only twenty of them to put in the contest. Once he had done that, he had to glue them carefully and neatly on some poster board. All his work paid off when he won first prize.

2. Which of the following is the best *summary* of the above story?
Ⓐ Steve had a hard time choosing what pictures to enter.
Ⓑ Steve carefully glued his pictures on poster board.
Ⓒ Steve took over a hundred pictures during the summer.
Ⓓ Steve's work paid off when he won first prize in a photo contest.

Go on to the next page.

Summarizing: Test 1, p. 2

When camping, people often make a fire to cook hot dogs and marshmallows. However, campers should be careful with fires. A fire should be built in a safe place. Some parks have pits in the ground or a circle of rocks in which campers can build a fire. Also, a fire should be watched at all times. A fire should not be left until it is completely out. If an uncontrolled fire is seen, it should be reported as soon as possible.

3. Which of the following is the best *summary* of the above story?
   Ⓐ Fires should be watched at all times and not be left until they are completely out.
   Ⓑ Report all campfires at once.
   Ⓒ Campfires should be built in pits or in a circle of rocks.
   Ⓓ Campers should be careful with campfires by building them in safe places and watching them carefully.

The class had been studying whales for the past two weeks. The teacher had told the class to write a report about their favorite whale. Tom chose to write about the blue whale. It was his favorite because it was the biggest whale. Ben decided to write about the killer whale. It was his favorite because he had seen one last summer.

4. Which of the following is the best *summary* of the above story?
   Ⓐ Tom wrote about the blue whale because it was the biggest one.
   Ⓑ The students wrote reports about their favorite animal.
   Ⓒ After studying about whales, the students wrote reports about their favorite whale.
   Ⓓ Ben saw a killer whale while on vacation last summer.

Sharon needed to get some toothpaste at the drugstore. Then she had to stop by the shoe repair shop and pick up her mother's shoes. Next, she was going to buy some seeds at the garden shop.

5. Which of the following is the best *summary* of the above story?
   Ⓐ Sharon needed to go to the garden shop.
   Ⓑ Sharon had several errands to do.
   Ⓒ Sharon was out of toothpaste.
   Ⓓ Sharon's shoes needed to be repaired.

Summarizing: Test 2

📖 **Read each story. Then read the answer choices.** ✏️ **Fill in the answer circle in front of the best summary of the story.**

Every morning I make my bed. When I come home from school, I set the table for dinner. After dinner, I help wash the dishes and put them away. Once a week, I dust the furniture and sweep the floor. Sometimes I help Mom fold clothes. My mom always says "thank you," because she likes it when I help out around the house.

1. Which of the following is the best *summary* of the above story?
   - Ⓐ Washing dishes is my favorite job.
   - Ⓑ Sometimes I fold clothes.
   - Ⓒ I do many things to help around the house.
   - Ⓓ Setting the table is fun after school.

After Jim crawled into his tent, he had a hard time falling asleep. There seemed to be a hundred rocks right under his sleeping bag. He was able to shift some of the large ones to the side. He knew he would have to move more of the rocks tomorrow. He finally fell asleep listening to the sounds of the woods.

2. Which of the following is the best *summary* of the above story?
   - Ⓐ Jim wasn't very comfortable, but he finally fell asleep.
   - Ⓑ Jim knew he should move some of the rocks.
   - Ⓒ Jim shifted some of the large rocks to the side.
   - Ⓓ Jim liked to listen to the sounds of the woods.

Go on to the next page.

Summarizing: Test 2, p. 2

Susan and Pam had a wonderful time at the park. They had played on the playground. They ate a picnic lunch that Susan's mother had packed for them. When they got home, they asked their mothers if they could go back to the park the following day.

3. Which of the following is the best *summary* of the above story?
- (A) Susan and Pam had such a good day in the park that they wanted to go the next day.
- (B) Susan's mother packed a picnic lunch for them to take to the park.
- (C) Both Susan's and Pam's mothers said the girls could go to the park again.
- (D) The girls liked playing on the swings the best.

Justin was a volunteer at the zoo. Sometimes he helped the zookeepers get the food ready for the animals. Other times he helped wash the dishes that the animals ate out of. His favorite times were when he got to hold one of the baby animals and give it a bottle.

4. Which of the following is the best *summary* of the above story?
- (A) As a zoo volunteer, Justin got to help with the animals.
- (B) Justin liked to feed the baby animals the best.
- (C) Zoo volunteers get to help zookeepers clean cages.
- (D) Zoo volunteers prepare the animals' food.

Cindy had told her parents many times that she was too old for a baby-sitter. She wished that they would realize that she was old enough to take care of herself. Then one night, there was a storm while her parents were away. The lights went out. She was glad that her baby-sitter was there. They had lighted some candles and waited until the lights came back on.

5. Which of the following is the best *summary* of the above story?
- (A) A storm made the electricity go off at Cindy's house.
- (B) Cindy found out she still wanted to have a baby-sitter.
- (C) Cindy thought she was too old for a baby-sitter.
- (D) Cindy's parents went out during a storm.

Unit Three: Test Taking
Summarizing 4, SV 2053-2

Summarizing: Test 3

📖 **Read each story. Then read the answer choices.** ✏️ **Fill in the answer circle in front of the best summary of the story.**

Carlos was finished decorating his holiday cards. He had bought paper and stickers. He had cut out designs and glued them on the cards. He had written something special in each one. Then he had put stamps on the envelopes and mailed them out. He could hardly wait until his friends and family opened them.

1. Which of the following is the best *summary* of the above story?
   Ⓐ Carlos had cut out and glued designs on cards.
   Ⓑ Carlos wrote special messages inside his holiday cards.
   Ⓒ Carlos had made holiday cards to send to his friends and family.
   Ⓓ Carlos was having fun making holiday cards.

A *design* is the arrangement of lines or shapes in ways that are pleasing to the eye. If you look around outside, you will see beautiful designs in nature. The shapes of flowers and leaves are designs. Frost on a window glass also makes a design. Butterfly wings usually have beautiful designs on them. Where else do you see designs in nature?

2. Which of the following is the best *summary* of the above story?
   Ⓐ Butterfly wings are beautiful.
   Ⓑ Nature is full of designs.
   Ⓒ Designs are fun to make in the snow.
   Ⓓ Frost on a window makes a design.

Go on to the next page.

Summarizing: Test 3, p. 2

A small lizard, called a gecko, has a special way of protecting itself. When attacked, it simply drops off its tail. The tail keeps wriggling on the ground, confusing attackers. Soon new cells will grow where the tail dropped off. This growth is called a bud. After about eight to twelve months, the gecko has a new, full-sized tail.

3. Which of the following is the best *summary* of the above story?
- Ⓐ It takes almost a year for a gecko to grow a new tail.
- Ⓑ Some animals like to eat geckos.
- Ⓒ A gecko is a kind of lizard.
- Ⓓ A gecko can make its tail drop off and grow a new one.

Ants are called social insects because they live and work together. Some of their nests have less than fifty ants, and some have thousands of ants. Their nests can be found under stones, in hollow stems, and in the ground. Usually their nests have more than one opening. The openings are sometimes hidden.

4. Which of the following is the best *summary* of the above story?
- Ⓐ Ants live in groups in a nest.
- Ⓑ Ants build their nests in the ground.
- Ⓒ An ant nest has several openings.
- Ⓓ Ants live and work together.

Penny and Rosita like to go swimming in the neighborhood pool. They play water tag and dive off the diving board. When they cannot get to the pool, they spray each other with a water hose. It cools them off on a hot day. Sometimes, Rosita's mom takes them to the ocean. That is their favorite place to swim.

5. Which of the following is the best *summary* of the above story?
- Ⓐ Penny and Rosita mainly swim in the neighborhood pool.
- Ⓑ Penny and Rosita like to play in water.
- Ⓒ Penny and Rosita like to swim in the ocean the best.
- Ⓓ Penny and Rosita play in water on cold days.

Summarizing: Test 4

📖 **Read each story. Then read the answer choices.** ✏️ **Fill in the answer circle in front of the best summary of the story.**

Dogs must be taken to a veterinarian for checkups and shots. They also must be fed and watered properly every day. Dogs need to be given an occasional bath. The owner of a dog must also make sure the dog gets enough exercise. In some places, dogs must wear a tag to say they have all their shots and are healthy.

1. Which of the following is the best *summary* of the above story?
   Ⓐ Dogs need a lot of care and attention.
   Ⓑ Dogs are expensive pets.
   Ⓒ Dogs need to be taken on walks every day.
   Ⓓ Dogs are the best kind of pets.

People, animals, and plants all need clean water to drink. Water also helps us keep ourselves, and everything else, clean. The best thing about water is how it feels when you jump into it on a hot summer day!

2. Which of the following is the best *summary* of the above story?
   Ⓐ Our bodies need a lot of water.
   Ⓑ Everything would be dirty if we did not have water.
   Ⓒ Swimming is fun on a hot summer day.
   Ⓓ Water is useful in many different ways.

Go on to the next page.

Summarizing: Test 4, p. 2

Opossums are amazing little animals. When a person finds an opossum, it may be putting on an act of being "dead." It's "playing possum." A person can tweak the opossum's whiskers or pull its toes, and there is no sign of life. The opossum doesn't seem to be breathing, and it's hard to find a heartbeat.

3. Which of the following is the best *summary* of the above story?
Ⓐ Opossums like to pretend to be dead.
Ⓑ Opossums act dead when people are near.
Ⓒ Opossums die when people come near.
Ⓓ An opossum can make its heartbeat slow down.

When the American Revolution began, the American colonies stopped using the English flag. Each one of the thirteen colonies used a different flag. This was so confusing that George Washington wrote to Congress and said, "Please fix some flag by which our vessels will know each other."

4. Which of the following is the best *summary* of the above story?
Ⓐ George Washington suggested that the colonies have one flag.
Ⓑ George Washington fought in the American Revolution.
Ⓒ Colonies used different flags during the American Revolution.
Ⓓ Using different flags confused George Washington.

A statue of Balto, the dog, stands in Central Park, New York. Balto was a sled dog who was part of the United States Postal Service in Alaska. In the winter of 1925, he carried a lifesaving medicine more than 600 miles during a blizzard to save children of Nome, Alaska.

5. Which of the following is the best *summary* of the above story?
Ⓐ Balto was a famous dog in New York.
Ⓑ Balto was a sled dog in Alaska who worked to deliver mail.
Ⓒ Balto was sick and needed medicine.
Ⓓ Balto was a sled dog who helped deliver medicine in a blizzard.

Summarizing: Test 5

📖 **Read each story. Then read the answer choices.** ✏️ **Fill in the answer circle in front of the best summary of the story.**

A mother robin perched on a tree branch. She had a worm in her beak. She looked down at her three baby birds. They all had their mouths open. They were making lots of noise because they were hungry. The mother robin gave the worm to one of her babies. She flew off again and came back with a small insect. She fed it to another baby bird. The mother robin made several trips to get food for the babies before they all fell asleep.

1. Which of the following is the best *summary* of the above story?
Ⓐ A mother robin fed her babies.
Ⓑ Baby robins ate worms.
Ⓒ A mother robin flew to and from the nest several times.
Ⓓ After eating, the baby robins went to sleep.

Maria decided to make a cake. She got all the ingredients out. Just then the phone rang. It was her friend Gail. They started talking. Before Maria knew it, she had been talking for over an hour! She said good-bye to Gail and went into the kitchen. She wanted to have the cake finished for her father before he got home.

2. Which of the following is the best *summary* of the above story?
Ⓐ Maria talked to her friend for over an hour.
Ⓑ Maria was making a cake for her father's birthday.
Ⓒ Maria talked for so long, she had to hurry to make the cake.
Ⓓ Maria's friend Gail called her on the phone.

Go on to the next page.

Summarizing: Test 5, p. 2

Jamie's uncle came to visit. Jamie took his uncle up to his room. Jamie wanted to show his uncle the new coins he had in his coin collection. He had gotten three new coins since his uncle had last visited. Jamie had a 1921 penny and a 1932 nickel. His favorite new coin was a 1902 dime.

3. Which of the following is the best *summary* of the above story?
Ⓐ Jamie's favorite coin was a 1902 dime.
Ⓑ Jamie had just gotten three new coins.
Ⓒ Jamie showed his uncle his new coins.
Ⓓ Jamie's uncle came to visit.

Cindy's cousin called and asked her to spend the weekend at her house. Cindy liked to go to her cousin's house. They always had lots of fun together. Cindy had a big school project due on Monday. She had most of the things she needed, but she knew it would take her a while to put it all together. She told her cousin that maybe she could come over next weekend.

4. Which of the following is the best *summary* of the above story?
Ⓐ Cindy always had fun at her cousin's house.
Ⓑ Cindy had a big school project due on Monday.
Ⓒ Cindy told her cousin she would visit this weekend.
Ⓓ Cindy had homework, so she couldn't go visit her cousin.

Sam took his dog to school. But this school wasn't for children. It was for dogs. With the help of special trainers, Sam was able to teach his dog to sit, come, lie down, and stay.

5. Which of the following is the best *summary* of the above story?
Ⓐ Sam's dog won a prize at school.
Ⓑ Sam took his dog to a school to learn to behave.
Ⓒ Sam's dog learned how to help blind people walk around town.
Ⓓ Sam took his dog to school for show and tell.

Summarizing to Improve Comprehension, Grade 4

Answer Key

p. 1 1. detail 2. detail 3. detail 4. summary 5. detail 6. summary 7. detail 8. detail

p. 2 1a. detail b. detail c. detail d. summary e. detail 2a. detail b. detail c. summary d. detail e. detail

p. 3 1. raptors 2. eyesight 3. talons 4. animals 5. migrate 6. hibernate 7. spring 8. young

p. 4 1. tornado 2. trees 3. towns 4. plains 5. warm 6. cold 7. thunderstorms

p. 5 1. Mark couldn't find his watch anywhere. 2. Allan likes to play many kinds of games. 3. Mrs. Johnson was a very caring person. 4. You never know where you'll find a bird nest!

p. 6 1. Boats move across the water in different ways. 2. One of the most common kinds of boats on a river is the barge. 3. Buoys are floating objects that help sailors and boaters steer safely through tricky waters near shore. 4. A houseboat is built more for living than for sailing.

p. 7 1. Underline: The seahorse is a fish that isn't anything like a fish.; a 2. Underline: The roadrunner is a flightless bird that eats rattlesnakes for dinner.; b

p. 8 1. Underline: Many accidents happen on sidewalks.; a 2. Underline: The alligator is sly when it comes to catching food.; b 3. Underline: A tree is a very useful plant.; b

p. 9 Answers may vary slightly. 1. clothes 2. salad 3. birds

p. 10 Answers may vary slightly. 1. mailed 2. cleaned 3. homework

p. 11 1. Bill 2. The story takes place in Bill's neighborhood. 3. Bill is trying to earn money to buy a football helmet.

p. 12 Answers may vary slightly. 1a. Mrs. Wilson; neighbors b. The story takes place at Mrs. Wilson's house. c. The neighbors gave Mrs. Wilson a surprise welcome home party. 2a. Greg b. The story takes place in Greg's bedroom. c. Greg was angry because his mother would not let him go to the movies without an adult.

p. 13 Answers may vary slightly. 1. Carl 2. The story takes place at Carl's new house. 3. Carl has moved into a new house and wants to meet some friends.

p. 14 Answers may vary slightly. 1a. Maureen b. The story takes place on a school bus. c. Maureen is going into fifth grade and is worried about being the youngest student in a new school. 2a. Mr. Clark b. The story takes place in Mr. Clark's classroom. c. Mr. Clark's students are giving him a surprise birthday party.

p. 15 Answer order may vary. A II. Types of mines III. Preparing coal IV. Ways of transporting coal B IA. Long ears IB. Sharp teeth IC. Strong hind legs IIA. Feed at night IIB. Kick and bite IIIA. Jackrabbit IIIB. Cottontail

p. 16 Answers may vary slightly. I. Choose a proper growing spot A. Fertile ground B. Sunshine C. Water II. Prepare the soil A. Scatter fertilizer B. Dig up ground C. Break up clumps D. Rake until level III. Plant some seeds A. Dig holes B. Place seeds equally C. Cover with soil D. Water the garden

p. 17 Answer order may vary: Rough pad under each toe; Pointed tips on toes; Short legs

p. 18 Answer order may vary: Kangaroo; Emu; Platypus; Koala

p. 19 Main character: Georgia; Setting: Georgia's house; Answers may vary. Plot: Georgia sees a shirt she wants., Georgia's sister will buy it for Georgia's birthday., Georgia's sister buys the wrong shirt., Georgia acts as if it is the right shirt.

p. 20 Main character: Ken and Phil; Setting: Ken's neighborhood; Answers may vary. Plot: Ken takes care of Phil the dog., Phil runs away., Phil comes back, but smells bad., Ken gives Phil a bath.

p. 21 Answers may vary. 1. Fox 2. woods 3. grapes 4. lunch 5. sour

p. 22 1. Romans 2. brows 3. handkerchiefs 4. wave 5. display 6. affection

p. 24 Answers may vary. 1. Ron was watching the animals during feeding time at the zoo. 2. Janet wanted to plant her vegetable garden, so she bought some seeds and planted them. 3. Diane had a very busy day planned, so she woke up early.

Summarizing 4, SV 2053-2

p. 25 Answers may vary. 1. Everyone asked Juanita how to spell words because she had won the spelling bee for several years. 2. Judy visits the meadow in all four seasons to see how it changes. 3. Paula's dog, Jupiter, can do many tricks.

p. 26 Answers may vary.1. Many animals make their home in the meadow. 2. Terry likes to read many kinds of books. 3. Wesley likes to help take care of his one-year-old sister. 4. Ana got many presents for her birthday.

p. 28 Answers may vary. Possible answer: Betty saw a house across the valley that looked very big and grand. When she and her father drove over to see it, the house did not seem so special. As she looked at her house across the way, it looked much bigger and more beautiful.

p. 29 Answers may vary. Web answers: In boots, In trees, Under rocks, In tents, In woodpiles, In backpacks; Summary: When camping, people can find spiders anywhere in nature. They can also find that spiders crawl into their clothing.

p. 30 Answers may vary. Web answers: Mammals, Fur, Wings, Sleeps upside down, Flies at night, Eats insects, Lives in colonies; Summary: Bats are flying mammals that live in colonies. They fly at night looking for insects to eat. When resting, they perch upside down.

p. 31 Main character: Miss Trinidad; Setting: In Miss Trinidad's house; Answers may vary. Plot: Miss Trinidad lost her glasses., She searched all over the house., She found the glasses on her head.; Summary: Miss Trinidad lost her glasses. After much searching in her house, she found the glasses on her head.

p. 32 Main character: Marilu and her grandfather; Setting: Marilu's house; Answers may vary. Plot: Marilu and her grandpa want to build a birdhouse for chickadees., They read a book., They ask a neighbor's advice., They watch the chickadees after the house is finished.; Summary: Marilu and her grandpa research how to build a birdhouse for chickadees. They read a book and ask a neighbor. Once finished, Marilu enjoys watching the birds.

p. 33 1. Lindsey and Kate 2. The story takes place at a mall. Answers may vary. 3. Lindsey and her friend go to the mall. They see many stores. They meet Lindsey's mom at 5:00.; Summary: Lindsey and her friend Kate go to the mall. They see many stores. They are having such a good time that they are surprised when it is time to meet Lindsey's mom.

p. 34 1. Megan 2. The story takes place at Megan's house. Answers may vary. 3. Megan wants a new tennis racket. She has some money saved from her allowance. To earn more, she cleans the garage and weeds the garden. Her parents give Megan more money. Megan goes to the store to buy the racket. Summary: Megan wants a new tennis racket. She has saved most of her allowance, but cleans the garage and weeds the garden to get the rest. Before long, Megan has all the money to buy the racket.

p. 35 1. Three goats and a troll 2. The story takes place on a bridge. Answers may vary. 3. Three goats try to cross a bridge to eat grass. A troll tries to stop each goat. He lets the smaller and middle goats pass. When the biggest goat crosses, the goat uses its horns to push the troll off the bridge.

p. 36 Check students' news article.

p. 37 1. B 2. D

p. 38 3. D 4. C 5. B

p. 39 1. C 2. A

p. 40 3. A 4. A 5. B

p. 41 1. C 2. B

p. 42 3. D 4. A 5. B

p. 43 1. A 2. D

p. 44 3. B 4. A 5. D

p. 45 1. A 2. C

p. 46 3. C 4. D 5. B